Andrew Woods

OXFORD GRAMMAR 2

T0342672

Name: _____

Class: _____

OXFORD
UNIVERSITY PRESS
AUSTRALIA & NEW ZEALAND

CONTENTS

TOPIC 1: NOUNS

TOPIC 2: ADJECTIVES, ARTICLES AND NOUN GROUPS

TOPIC 3: VERBS, ADVERBS AND PHRASES

OXFORD UNIVERSITY PRESS

History
Secrets

The Gobbles

Tick likes toys.

Tock likes sport.

Tim likes music.

Tam likes pets.

Bip likes food.

Bop likes Bip.

Toys, sport, music, pets and *food* are names of things.

Naming words are called nouns.

Look at the pictures and write:

1 three nouns that are toys that Tick likes.

_____

2 three nouns that are sports that Tock likes.

_____

3 three nouns that are musical instruments that Tim likes.

_____

4 three nouns that are pets that Tam likes.

_____

5 three nouns that are foods that Bip likes.

_____

6 Who does Bop like?

_____

NOW TRY THIS!

Write the names of three foods that you like to eat.

_____

_____

_____

The Gobbles go bush

The Gobbles are on a camping trip in the bush.

OXFORD UNIVERSITY PRESS

Nouns that name people, animals and things are called common nouns. *Woman*, *beach*, *fish* and *axe* are all common nouns.

1 Find the 11 Gobbles in the picture. Use common nouns to complete these sentences about the Gobbles.

a I am being chased by a _____.

b I'm crawling into a _____.

c I'm in a _____ on the _____.

Remember: Nouns are naming words.

d I'm inside the _____ reading a _____.

e Can you see me behind the _____?

2 Use words from the box to complete the sentences below.

> plants   places   animals   things

a **Tent**, **lamp**, **pot** and **fire** name _____.

b **Wombat**, **bird**, **snake** and **emu** name _____.

c **Tree**, **flower**, **fern** and **bush** name _____.

d **Home**, **school**, **town** and **forest** name _____.

NOW TRY THIS!

Find five common nouns in the picture that haven't already been named.

_____

_____

_____

_____

_____

Dear Gobble

The Gobbles are holding letters that have come in today's mail.

Tick Tock
22 Mucky Road
Smelly Sock 0303

Tock Tuck
5 Spotty Lane
Unmade Bed 0203

Tim Tum
6 Grime Street
Messy Toybox 0103

Tam Tim
9 Untidy Road
Muddle City 0403

Bip Bip
20 Dusty Highway
Litterville 0304

Bop Aloola
15 Jumble Road
Clutterberry 0340

OXFORD UNIVERSITY PRESS

Tom, Kim and Saleem are the names of people. Baker Street, Richmond and Queensland are the names of places.

The names of people and places are called proper nouns.
Proper nouns start with a capital letter.

1 These proper nouns for people and places should start with a capital letter. Write them correctly. Look at the letters on page 8 to help you.

The names of people, places and things are called proper nouns. They begin with a capital letter.

grime street _____   tock tuck _____

muddle city _____   tick tack _____

tam tim _____   jumble road _____

2 Write the proper nouns.

a Where does Tick Tack live? _____

_____

b Who lives in Grime Street? _____

c Who lives in Clutterberry? _____

NOW TRY THIS!

Add proper nouns to show who the letters were sent to.

a Tam Tim sent a letter to a Gobble who lives in Smellysock.

She sent a letter to _____.

b Bip Bip sent a letter to a Gobble who lives in Spotty Lane.

She sent a letter to _____.

c Bop Aloola sent a letter to someone at number 20.

He sent a letter to _____.

Read these poems with your teacher.

Solomon Grundy

Solomon Grundy
Born on Monday
Christened on Tuesday
Married on Wednesday
Took ill on Thursday
Worse on Friday
Died on Saturday
Buried on Sunday ...

Months

January scorching
February hot.
March starts cooling down
To April's mixed pot.
May leaves are colouring
June showers begin.
July winds are chilly
And August keeps us in.
September rains fall lightly
October life anew.
November warms us up again
For December's things to do.

OXFORD UNIVERSITY PRESS

The names of the days and the months are proper nouns.

1 The names of days are proper nouns. They begin with a capital letter.

Write some days of the week using the poem about Solomon Grundy to help you.

_____

_____

2 The names of the months are proper nouns. They begin with a capital letter.

Write some months using the poem 'Months' to help you.

_____

_____

Did you begin these proper nouns with capital letters?

3 The names of people are proper nouns. They begin with a capital letter.

a Write your name here. _____

b Write a friend's name here. _____

c Write the name of someone famous here. _____

_____

NOW TRY THIS!

On a piece of paper write a list of proper nouns for people in your family. Next to each person's name, write the month in which they have their birthday.

Insects and spiders

It is easy to tell the difference between flying insects and spiders when we look at a diagram with labels showing their different parts.

Parts of an insect

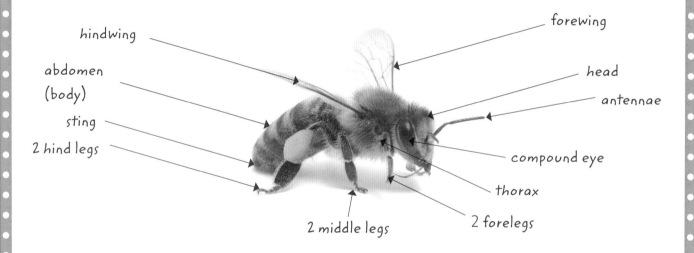

hindwing

abdomen (body)

sting

2 hind legs

2 middle legs

forewing

head

antennae

compound eye

thorax

2 forelegs

Parts of a spider

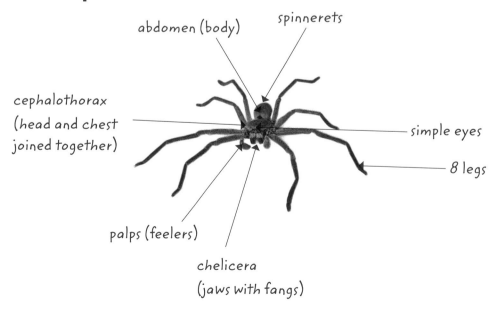

abdomen (body)

spinnerets

cephalothorax (head and chest joined together)

simple eyes

8 legs

palps (feelers)

chelicera (jaws with fangs)

OXFORD UNIVERSITY PRESS

Some nouns are everyday names for people, places and things.
Some nouns are technical names often used in science topics.
Many of the words that label the diagrams of the insect and spider are technical nouns. They are sometimes called scientific nouns.

1 Replace these everyday nouns with technical nouns from the diagram of a flying insect on page 12.

a feelers _____

b back wing _____

c front wing _____

d body _____

2 Write nouns from page 12 to fill the gaps in these sentences.

a A spider has eight l_____.

b An insect's legs are joined to its t_____.

c Spiders have simple _____ but _____ have compound eyes.

d S_____ are used by a spider to spin its web.

NOW TRY THIS!

Use the diagrams to help you explain how flying insects and spiders are different. Include technical and everyday nouns.

_____

_____

_____

_____

The Gobbles' goblets

Here are the Gobbles' goblets. The goblets contain magic potions.

HONESTY

BRAVERY

FEAR

WEALTH

HUMOUR

STRENGTH

OXFORD UNIVERSITY PRESS

Some nouns name people, places, animals and things that we can see and touch.

Some nouns name ideas or feelings. We cannot see or touch these things.

Can you say which goblet each of these Gobbles drank a magic potion from?

Abstract nouns are names for ideas or feelings.

 1 Tim likes to tell jokes. _____

 2 Bip always tells the truth. _____

 3 Tick can lift a heavy weight. _____

 4 Tam wants to fight dragons. _____

 **5** Tock is rich beyond belief. _____

 6 Bop is afraid of the dark. _____

NOW TRY THIS!

These goblets contain GOOD potions and BAD potions.

Tick the goblets with GOOD potions. Cross out the goblets with BAD potions.

 EVIL  HAPPINESS  PEACE  ANGER  HURT  LOVE

Masked rhymes

Read these rhymes with your teacher.
(They may seem strange to read until you finish the activities on page 17.)

An elephant living in Kent

Had a nose that was terribly bent.

The elephant followed his nose

One day I suppose

And no one knows which way the elephant went.

The grand old Duke of York,

The grand old Duke of York had ten thousand men;

The grand old Duke of York marched
    the ten thousand men up to the top of the hill,

And the grand old Duke of York marched
    the ten thousand men down again!

And when the ten thousand men were up
    the ten thousand men were up,

And when the ten thousand men were down
    the ten thousand men were down;

And when the ten thousand men were only
    halfway up,

The ten thousand men were neither up nor down.

OXFORD UNIVERSITY PRESS

Sometimes it is better to use a **pronoun** than to repeat a name (**noun**).

1 Read the rhymes on page 16. Use different colours to colour the words that name people, places, animals and things.

2 Use **pronouns** from the boxes to make the rhymes easier to read.

> He   he

Pronouns can be used in place of nouns for people, places, animals and things.

a An elephant living in Kent

Had a nose that was terribly bent,

_____ followed his nose

One day I suppose

And no one knows which way _____ went.

> they   He   they   They   them   they
>
> He   they   them   they   he

b The grand old Duke of York,

_____ had ten thousand men;

_____ marched _____ up to the top of the hill,

And _____ marched _____ down again!

And when _____ were up _____ were up,

And when _____ were down _____ were down;

And when _____ were only halfway up,

_____ were neither up nor down.

Tiddalik
(an Aboriginal story)

Read with your teacher.

Tiddalik was the largest frog ever known. One morning he woke up very thirsty. He was so thirsty he drank all the creeks, billabongs, rivers and lakes dry.

Tiddalik drank until there was no fresh water left anywhere.

Soon all the animals would die of thirst.

The animals decided that if they could make Tiddalik laugh, perhaps the water in his belly would spill out.

Kookaburra told jokes. Tiddalik did not laugh.

The kangaroos jumped over Tiddalik's head, but he did not laugh.

The emus ran around Tiddalik in a silly way. The frog still would not laugh.

Frilled lizard ran on two legs with her frill flapping, but Tiddalik still would not laugh.

The eels started to dance. They swayed and wriggled until they had tied themselves into knots.

Tiddalik smiled.

Tiddalik grinned.

Then Tiddalik laughed . . . and laughed . . . and laughed. He laughed so much that the water in his belly gushed out.

Soon, all was well again, and the animals were no longer thirsty.

OXFORD UNIVERSITY PRESS

Nouns that tell us more than one are called plural nouns.

1 To change these nouns to plural nouns just add **s**.

a creek _____

b river _____

c billabong _____

d eel _____

e knot _____

f kangaroo _____

2 Write plural nouns to describe each picture.

a

_____

b

_____

c

_____

d

_____

To make some nouns plural nouns we must add es.

3 Add **es** to make these plural nouns.

a dish_____

b stitch_____

c fox_____

d dress_____

e beach_____

f lunch_____

g kiss_____

h buzz_____

i bus_____

NOW TRY THIS!

Sometimes, we change the spelling to show a noun as more than one. These are called irregular plural nouns.

Can you write these nouns as plural nouns?

a mouse _____

b child _____

c tooth _____

TOPIC 1: TEST YOURSELF!

Nouns and pronouns

1 Shade the bubble next to the common noun.

  ○ running   ○ Victoria   ○ bird   ○ yellow

2 Shade the bubble below the common noun in this sentence.

Nick kicked the football.
   ○   ○   ○   ○

3 Shade the bubble next to the proper noun.

  ○ April   ○ may   ○ catch   ○ book

4 Shade the bubble below the proper noun in this sentence.

We went for a drive on Sunday.
  ○ ○   ○   ○

5 Shade the bubble next to the pronoun that completes this sentence.

Mum said I couldn't go out to play until _____ cleaned my room.

  ○ it   ○ her   ○ me   ○ I

6 Shade the bubble next to the pronoun that completes this sentence.

Evie and I were hot so _____ went for a swim in the river.

  ○ it   ○ us   ○ we   ○ me

OXFORD UNIVERSITY PRESS

7 On a piece of paper, write the proper nouns for the days of the week.

8 Here are some characters from a story. Make up proper nouns for each character. Write their names under their pictures.

_____   _____   _____

_____   _____

9 Shade the bubble next to the plural noun.

○ flower   ○ flowers   ○ flour   ○ flow

HOW AM I DOING?

Colour the boxes if you understand.

Common nouns name ordinary things. ☐

The names of people and places are called proper nouns. ☐

Pronouns can take the place of common or proper nouns. ☐

Plural nouns show more than one. ☐

More about the Gobbles

Read with your teacher.

Gobbles are odd little imps.

They wear funny suits that look like pyjamas.

Sometimes Gobbles wear large, floppy, red hats.

Sometimes they wear small, pointy, blue caps.

Gobbles' clothes are always colourful.

Gobbles live in strange places too.

Some Gobbles live in messy, unmade beds.

Some Gobbles live in untidy, muddled drawers.

Even one old, smelly sock lying on the bedroom floor can make a cosy home for a Gobble.

Gobbles are very shy. The only way you can see a Gobble is to keep your bedroom tidy.

The Gobbles will soon make it messy again for they need somewhere to live.

Whenever Mum and Dad ask, "Why is your room so messy?", you can say, "Oh no! I've got those pesky Gobbles again!"

OXFORD UNIVERSITY PRESS

Some words tell us more about people and things. They describe the colour, shape, size or number of things.
For example: **red** *hat*, **round** *ball*, **big** *nose*, **two** *clowns*
Red, *round*, *big* and *two* describe a hat, a ball, a nose and some clowns.

Read about the Gobbles with your teacher.

Words that describe a noun are called adjectives.

1 Draw circles around the words that describe the words in *italics*.

a *Gobbles*	odd smelly little floor six	
	strange wear messy shy	
b *beds*	messy hats imps unmade	
c *sock*	floor old one homes smelly	
d *Gobbles' clothes*	funny colourful sometimes room	
e *hats*	pyjamas floppy large little red	
f *caps*	small pointy wear they blue	
g *drawers*	muddled live untidy Gobble	

2 On a piece of paper, draw a Gobble in a funny, colourful suit wearing a large, floppy hat or a small, pointy cap.

NOW TRY THIS!

Write words to describe:

a a monster _____

b a puppy _____

c a racing car _____

d a flower _____

The falcon and the boy

Read the story about the falcon and the boy with your teacher.

A beautiful falcon once found herself caught in a deadly trap.

A young boy, who was passing close by, saw how sad the magnificent bird was to be trapped. He helped to set the miserable bird free.

Quickly the falcon flew up into the safe branches of a tall gum tree.

Happy to have been helpful, the boy sat down below an old, stone wall to eat his tasty lunch.

With her sharp eyesight the falcon could see that the unsafe wall was about to crumble.

She swooped from the tree and snatched up the startled boy's woollen cap.

The angry lad leapt up and chased the bird. As he did, the crumbly wall tumbled to the ground right where the boy had been sitting.

The grateful bird had repaid the thankful boy for his earlier kindness.

OXFORD UNIVERSITY PRESS

Adjectives tell us more about nouns (naming words). They describe people, places, animals and things.

She wore a **purple** *hat on a* **sunny** *day.*

Purple describes the hat. Sunny describes the day.

1 Write three adjectives from the story that describe:

a the boy _____

b the falcon _____

c the wall _____

2 Write adjectives from the story that describe the following:

a the bird's eyesight   s_____

b the boy's lunch   t_____

c the trap   d_____

d the boy's cap   w_____

e the tree   t_____   g_____

Use adjectives to make your writing more interesting.

NOW TRY THIS!

Add **ful** to these words to make new words that are adjectives.

For example: **colour + ful = colourful**

help _____   thank _____   care _____

pain _____   beauty _____(change the **y** to **i** first)

Read the next page **before** you fill in the gaps below.

the _____

the _____

the _____

a _____

a _____

a _____

an _____

an _____

an _____

the _____

a _____

an _____

OXFORD UNIVERSITY PRESS

Sometimes we use **the** before a noun.

For example: **the** *coat*, **the** *duck*, **the** *ape*, **the** *egg*, **the** *oak tree*, **the** *ugly witch*

1 Write **the** before these words.

a _____ book
b _____ cow
c _____ apple

d _____ house
e _____ eye
f _____ orange

When we add **the**, **a** or **an** before a noun (a naming word), we create a noun group. A noun group is a group of words that tell who or what the sentence is about.

We use an before a noun that begins with a vowel sound. Letters that make a vowel sound are a e i o u.

2 Write **a** before these words to make noun groups.

a _____ book
b _____ cow
c _____ plan

d _____ house
e _____ creek
f _____ tree

3 Write **an** before these words to make noun groups.

a _____ apple
b _____ eye
c _____ itch

d _____ orange
e _____ umbrella
f _____ axe

4 Write these nouns on the page opposite to make noun groups.

> ant   arm   clown   egg   onion   leaf   man
> old man   snail   star   truck   umbrella

NOW TRY THIS!

Some words begin with a vowel that does not make a short vowel sound. You should use **a** (not **an**) before these words. For example: **a unit** not **an unit**. Write **a** or **an** before these words or groups of words.

_____uniform   _____one-way street   _____egg

_____unicorn   _____umpire   _____octopus

Who or what?

Look at each picture carefully and then follow the instructions on the next page to answer the questions.

OXFORD UNIVERSITY PRESS

We can use adjectives (describing words) and articles (**a**, **an** or **the**) to make nouns more interesting. For example:

article   adjectives   noun

the   tiny   green   frogs

We call these groups of words noun groups. They tell us who or what the sentence or picture is about.

1 On page 28, write your own noun groups to match the pictures by using articles and adjectives from the box.

> an empty   an angry   a sleepy   the hairy
>
> the tall   a funny   a strong   the fast

2 Underline the noun group in each sentence below. To find the noun group, ask who or what the sentence is about.

a The fierce lion roared loudly.

b An old house fell down.

c Suddenly a terrible shark swam by.

3 In the box on the right, draw a strange animal with large eyes, an egg-shaped nose, two long arms and a prickly tail.

NOW TRY THIS!

Use these noun groups to help you draw an interesting picture on a piece of paper. Draw:

- five green balls
- a happy clown
- a red face
- blue wings
- a magic wand
- an impish fairy

Happy Diwali!

Read with your teacher.

Diwali is an important festival. It began in India but is today celebrated all around the world.

Diwali takes place every year and lasts for five wonderful days.

The word Diwali is sometimes called Deepavali or Divali. It means 'row of lights'.

Diwali is a time for colourful costumes, sparkling fireworks, twinkling lights, decorated homes and delicious foods.

During Diwali, families dress in bright, new clothes and then exchange special gifts and yummy sweets.

At Diwali time people make beautiful patterns on the floor using colourful powders and pretty flowers. This is called 'rangoli'.

Diwali is such a joyful festival for adults and children alike.

OXFORD UNIVERSITY PRESS

Adjectives are words that describe nouns.

1 Use the information on page 30 to help you write adjectives to describe these nouns.

a _____ costumes   b _____ lights

c _____ fireworks   d _____ foods

e _____ gifts   f _____ sweets

g _____ flowers   h _____ homes

2 Write three adjectives from the information on page 30 that end with -ful.

a _____

b _____

c _____

3 Make these adjectives opposites by changing -ful to -less.

For example: *colourful – colourless*

a useful _____   b careful _____

c joyful _____   d cheerful _____

NOW TRY THIS!

Write adjectives of your own that describe this Diwali costume.

_____

_____

_____

_____

TOPIC 2: TEST YOURSELF!

Adjectives, articles and noun groups

1 Shade the bubble next to the adjective describing size.

○ horse   ○ blue   ○ large   ○ find

2 Shade the bubble next to the adjective describing shape.

○ orange   ○ round   ○ nose   ○ house

3 Shade the bubble next to the number adjective.

○ hour   ○ second   ○ black   ○ window

4 Shade the bubble next to the adjective describing colour.

○ orange   ○ large   ○ first   ○ angry

5 Shade the bubble below the adjective in this sentence.

Tuesday was a windy day.
○   ○   ○   ○

6 Shade the bubble below the article in this sentence.

We saw a movie yesterday.
○   ○   ○   ○

OXFORD UNIVERSITY PRESS

7 Shade the bubble next to the noun group.

- ○ under the bridge
- ○ over the hill
- ○ a red tent
- ○ use their paws

8 Shade the bubble next to the noun group that would best complete this sentence.

The sad dragon lived alone in _____.

- ○ an angry sister
- ○ the busy street
- ○ a dark cave
- ○ the sharp teeth

9 Shade the bubble next to the noun group that would best fit the picture.

- ○ an old house
- ○ a sloppy lick
- ○ a fast car
- ○ the grey clouds

HOW AM I DOING?

Colour the boxes if you understand.

An adjective describes a noun. ☐

We can use the articles *the, a* or *an* before nouns. ☐

Noun groups tell us who or what the sentence is about. ☐

Mix a pancake

Mix a pancake,
Stir a pancake,
Pop it in the pan.
Fry the pancake,
Toss the pancake,
Catch it if you can.

Christina Rossetti

Fish and bird

How happy to be a fish,
To dive and skim,
To dart and float and swim
And play.
How happy to be a bird,
To fly and sing,
To glide on feathered wing
All day.

Rosemary Brinckman

Trees are swaying ...

Trees are swaying in the breeze,
Waves are tossing on the seas.
Bees are humming through the air,
Bugs are flitting here and there.
Birdies in their nests do sing
"Joy to this first day of Spring".

AjW

OXFORD UNIVERSITY PRESS

Some words tell us what is happening. We call these **verbs** or doing words.

1 Use the 'Mix a pancake' poem to write six **verbs** that tell us what to do with a pancake.

_____ it, _____ it,

_____ it, _____ it,

_____ it, _____ it.

2 Use the 'Trees are swaying ...' poem to help you write **verbs** that tell us what these things are doing.

For example: Trees <u>are swaying</u>_____ .

a Waves _____ .

b Bees _____ .

c Bugs _____ .

d Birdies _____ .

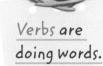

Verbs are
doing words.

3 Use the 'Fish and bird' poem to help you write:

a ... some things that fish can do.

_____

b ... some things that a bird can do.

_____

NOW TRY THIS!

Write **verbs** to tell us how these animals move. For example:

a worm wriggles.

a frog _____   a snake _____   a snail _____

a horse _____   a kitten _____   an eagle _____

The Gobbles at play

OXFORD UNIVERSITY PRESS

Do you remember?
Some words tell us what is being done. These words are called verbs.

1 Look at the picture opposite. It shows the Gobbles playing. Write a list of verbs telling what the Gobbles are doing in the picture.

For example: *hitting, swimming, batting, splashing*

_____

_____

_____

_____

_____

_____

_____

_____

2 Write four verbs to tell what you might do at a Sports Day.

_____   _____

_____   _____

NOW TRY THIS!

Write some verbs that tell what you might do while you are on holiday.

For example: **swim**, **play**

_____

_____

Verbs showing characters' actions, reactions, speech and thought processes

The Gobbles at playtime

Tick whistles when he walks.

Tock roars when she runs.

Tim hoots and howls when he swings.

Tam squeals and squawks when she slides.

Bip sings and laughs when she skips.

Bop moans and groans when he is kept in.

OXFORD UNIVERSITY PRESS

Some verbs tell us what is being **done**. For example: He *walked*.

Some verbs tell us what is being **said** or **thought**. For example: They *laughed*. She *shouted*. We *thought*.

Read the story about the Gobbles with your teacher.

1 What does Tick do when he walks? _____

2 What does Tock do when she runs? _____

3 What does Tim do when he swings?

_____ and _____

4 What does Tam do when she slides?

_____ and _____

5 What does Bip do when she skips?

_____ and _____

6 What does Bop do when he is kept in?

_____ and _____

7 What does Bop wish when he is kept in?

_____

NOW TRY THIS!

Write words from the story to finish these groups of verbs.

ran, running, _____   skipped, skipping, _____

swing, swinging, _____   walked, walking, _____

slid, sliding, _____   keep, keeping, _____

In the Gobbles' kitchen

The Gobbles are cooking today!

Tim is busily chopping the carrots.

Tick will finish peeling the potatoes soon.

Bip has eagerly rushed outside to pick some herbs.

Tock carefully removes the stockpot from the stove before it spills everywhere.

Downstairs, Tam is washing the dishes.

Bop waits hungrily near the table.

OXFORD UNIVERSITY PRESS

Some words tell us where, when and how something is happening.

Use words from the story on page 40 to answer these questions.

1 When are the Gobbles cooking? _____

2 Where is Tam washing the dishes? _____

3 How is Tim chopping the carrots? _____

4 Where might the stockpot spill? _____

5 When should Tock take the stockpot off the stove? She should remove the pot _____ it spills.

6 How should Tock take the stockpot off the stove?

_____

7 How did Bip rush? _____

8 Where is Bop waiting? _____

9 How is Bop waiting? _____

Adverbs tell us where, when and how an action takes place.

NOW TRY THIS!

Write whether these words tell where, when or how something might happen. For example: **after** tells **when**.

often _____   kindly _____   always _____

inside _____   quietly _____   under _____

Bop goes to the shop

Bop's mum asked him to go to the shop for some bread.

Bop walks to the shop.

Bop meets Tick. Tick lets Bop ride on his skateboard.

Bop meets Tock. They kick a footy in the park.

Bop meets Tim. Tim lets Bop sail his remote-controlled boat around the pond.

Bop meets Bip. Bop helps Bip put a roof on her cubby.

Bop meets Tam. She is in her billy-cart. Bop gives her a push.

At the shop Bop meets his mum. She is waiting ... FOR THE BREAD!

OXFORD UNIVERSITY PRESS

Some groups of words tell us where, when and how.
These groups of words are called phrases. For example:
The dog is on the mat. Where is the dog? On the mat.

Phrases can tell us when, where and how things happen.

1 Read 'Bop goes to the shop'. Answer each question below with a phrase telling where.

For example: Where did Bop walk? <u>to the shop</u>

a Where did Tick let Bop ride? _____

b Where did Bop and Tock kick a footy? _____

c Where did Bop sail Tim's boat? _____

d Where was Tam when Bop met her? _____

e Where did Bop's mum meet Bop? _____

2 Write a phrase to answer these questions about you.

a Where do you sleep? _____

b Where do you do your school work? _____

c How do you get outside? _____

d Where do you wear your hat? _____

e Where do you watch your favourite TV show? _____

NOW TRY THIS!

Read 'Bop goes to the shop' again. Write phrases that tell **why** Bop went to the shop and **why** his mum was waiting?

for _____

for _____

Preppo Boy

a Preppo Boy stands

b Preppo Boy flies

c Preppo Boy dives

d Preppo Boy skims

e Preppo Boy zooms

f Preppo Boy crashes

g Preppo Boy rushes

h Preppo Boy mends

OXFORD UNIVERSITY PRESS

Phrases (groups of words) tell us where, when and how something is happening.

1 Write these phrases where they belong in the story of Preppo Boy.

over the houses   under the bridge   to the hospital

in his bed   above the clouds   around the tree

into the wall   on the rock

2 Add words from the box to complete the phrases below.

under   at   before   with   after   during

a _____ six o'clock

b _____ a hammer

c _____ the thunderstorm

d _____ my birthday

e _____ the holidays

f _____ the bridge

> The short word that begins a phrase is called a preposition (say prep– oh–zi–shun).

NOW TRY THIS!

Write phrases that tell where you think that Preppo Boy might fly when he is well again.

a Preppo Boy flies _____.

b Preppo Boy flies _____.

c Preppo Boy flies _____.

Preppo Boy returns

Somebody needs help! They are lost in the forest.

Preppo Boy flies quickly into the sky.

He flies over clouds. He flies under clouds.

Preppo Boy flies into the forest.

He flies around a tree.

He flies around another tree.

He flies around another tree.

He flies around another tree.

And another, until soon . . .

Preppo Boy is lost in the forest too!

OXFORD UNIVERSITY PRESS

Do you remember?

Phrases tell us where, when and how something is happening.

For example: *The kite was stuck **in the tree**.* (where)

*I am going to the dentist **on Monday**.* (when)

1 Write four places where Preppo Boy flies.

a around _____ **b** into _____

c over _____ **d** under _____

2 Make four sentences matching the words from box A with words from boxes B and C to tell: who or what? did what? where?

For example: The little boy ran to the shop.

A Who or what? (noun, pronoun or noun group)	B Did what? (verb)	C Where? (phrase)
We	sailed	in the corner.
Jack Horner	sat	over the rock.
The spaceship	flew	in the boat.
The little lizard	crawled	around the Moon.

a _____

b _____

c _____

d _____

NOW TRY THIS!

Write a sentence of your own. Include a phrase telling where or when.

_____

_____

Flags

Read with your teacher.

The Aboriginal flag

Black represents the Aboriginal people.

The yellow circle represents the Sun.
To the Aboriginal people the Sun gives
us life and protects us.

Red represents the red earth and red ochre.
Red ochre is used in ceremonies to show the Aboriginal people's
connection to the land.

The Aboriginal flag was designed by Aboriginal artist Harold
Thomas and was first flown in Adelaide in 1971.

The Torres Strait Islander flag

Green represents the land.

The black strips represent the people
of the Torres Strait Islands.

Blue represents the sea.

White represents peace.

The five-pointed star represents the five main island groups
of the Torres Strait Islands.

The Dhari is the traditional headdress worn by the people
of the Torres Strait Islands.

The Torres Strait Islander flag was designed by Bernard Namok.

OXFORD UNIVERSITY PRESS

Verbs are words that tell us what has been done, is being done or will be done.

1 Use verbs from the box to complete the following sentences.

> protects   represents   worn   gives

a The Sun _____ us life.

b The Sun _____ us.

c The headdress is _____ by the people of the Torres Strait Islands.

d The yellow circle _____ the Sun.

Adverbs tell us more about verbs.

2 Use adverbs from the box to complete the sentences below.

> widely   often   proudly   first

a The flag is flown _____ by Aboriginal Australians.

b The Aboriginal flag was _____ flown in Adelaide.

c The flag is _____ recognised as a symbol of Australia's Aboriginal people.

d The flags are _____ flown next to the Australian flag.

NOW TRY THIS!

Use phrases of your own to complete these sentences.

a The little boy was lost_____.

b Today we are playing the game _____.

c We stopped _____ to buy milk and bread.

OXFORD UNIVERSITY PRESS

TOPIC 3: TEST YOURSELF!

Verbs, adverbs and phrases

1 Shade the bubble next to the verb.

○ tree   ○ jog   ○ under   ○ quickly

2 Shade the bubble below the verb in this sentence.

The eagle swooped from the sky.
   ○   ○   ○   ○

3 Shade the bubble next to the verb.

○ over the road   ○ on Tuesday
○ is walking   ○ the yellow banana

4 Shade the bubble below the adverb that tells **when**.

Tim walked to school today.
   ○   ○   ○   ○

5 Shade the bubble below the adverb that tells **where**.

"Put your bags there, please," said Mr Parker.
   ○   ○   ○   ○

6 Shade the bubble below the adverb that tells **how**.

Kate calmly picked up the spider.
   ○   ○   ○   ○

OXFORD UNIVERSITY PRESS

7 Shade the bubble next to the word that would best complete this sentence.

We found her hiding _____ *the cubby.*

○ from   ○ through   ○ inside   ○ between

8 Shade the bubble next to the group of words that is **not** a phrase.

○ in the forest   ○ we sailed

○ at 9 o'clock   ○ on Friday

9 Write your own phrases to complete these sentences about the pictures.

Preppo Boy flew _____

_____ .

Tam is sleeping _____

_____ .

A monster was standing _____

_____ .

HOW AM I DOING?

Colour the boxes if you understand.

Verbs are doing words that tell us about action. ☐

Adverbs tell us more about verbs. They tell us where, when and how. ☐

Phrases are groups of words that tell us where, when and how. ☐

Spud's bone

Read with your teacher.

Spud was on his way home through the park.
He spotted a big bone under a bush.

"Yum!" the dog thought. "I'll take that home with me."

Spud picked the bone up in his mouth and, happy
with his find, he trotted off along the path.

Soon Spud met Molly. "Can I share your
bone, Spud?" she asked.

"No way!" said Spud. "It's all for me." And
off he trotted. Next Spud met Hank.

"Can I share your bone, Spud?" he asked.

"No way!" said Spud. "It's all for me." Off he trotted once more.

Spud came to the grassy bank of a lake. He stopped and in the
clear water he saw a dog with a bone as big as his own.

"Yum!" he thought. "Two bones are better than one."

He went to snatch the bone from the other dog but,
when he opened his mouth, his own bone fell out.

SPLASH! Into the lake it tumbled and slowly
sank to the bottom.

Silly Spud had been looking at his own reflection
and now the greedy dog has no bones at all.

OXFORD UNIVERSITY PRESS

Different words can be used about the same thing. They belong together. The dog, Spud, he, and the greedy dog are all about the same thing. They can often be used in place of each other.

1 Read the story again. Colour all the words that are about the same thing: the main character, Spud.

2 Which groups do these nouns belong to? Place the following words in the table below to show which group they belong to.

elephant	train	monkey	cloak
teacher	pants	clown	coat
truck	farmer	lizard	dog
shirt	hat	wombat	doctor
car	queen	tram	ferry

We can often group words together because they are all about the same thing.

Animals	People	Clothes
Transport		

"Line up, you Gobbles!"

Tick   Tock   Tim   Tam Bip Bop

a

b

c

d

e

f

g

h

OXFORD UNIVERSITY PRESS

Some words are opposites.

Antonym (say an-tow-nim) is another word for opposite.

1 Look at the top picture on page 54.

The Gobbles are lining up at the school canteen. Finish the sentences below with opposites from the box.

> empty   sitting   last   long   shut   pulling

a Tick is first but Bop is _____.

b Tock is standing but Tim is _____.

c Tick's cup is full but Tock's cup is _____.

d Bip's scarf is short and Tam's scarf is _____.

e Bop is pushing and Tam is _____.

f Window A is open but Window B is _____.

2 Use the bottom pictures on page 54 to help you write opposites.

a night _____

b front _____

c go _____

d short _____

e poor _____

f young _____

g right _____

h dirty _____

NOW TRY THIS!

Can you write opposites for these words?

here _____

good _____

high _____

over _____

The Gobbles' night out

Tick yells.

Tock shouts.

Tim howls.

Tam squeals.

Bip screams.

Bop screeches.

It's time for the concert to begin.

Here come the Gobbles' favourite rock band.

They sing, they dance, they tell jokes, they look fantastic — yes it's …

Sonny Daze and the Bright Lights!

Thank you! Thank you very much!

OXFORD UNIVERSITY PRESS

Some words mean the same or nearly the same as other words.

1 Circle the words in each group that mean the same or nearly the same as the word in *italics*.

a *thin*   skinny   fat   large   slim

b *quick*   slow   fast   speedy   happy

c *look*   see   peep   loud   bang

d *dish*   dim   sing   funny   bowl

e *boat*   ship   cart   road   band

f *cry*   wash   sob   sing   weep

Words that mean the same or nearly the same are called synonyms (say sin-oh-nims).

2 Write six words that tell us what the Gobbles did at the concert.

_____   _____   _____

_____   _____   _____

3 Draw lines to match each word from the box with the group of words that mean the same or nearly the same.

a black   dim   murky   sooty   inky

b street   track   highway   lane   avenue

c bowl   plate   basin   saucer

dish

dark

road

NOW TRY THIS!

On another piece of paper, write your own words that mean the same or nearly the same as these words: **run**, **big**, **laugh**.

That's nonsense!

The tickle rhyme

"Who's that tickling my
back?" said the wall.
"Me," said a small
            Caterpillar.
               "I'm learning
               To crawl."

Ian Serraillier

Giraffes

Giraffes they are quite funny chaps
their necks so long and thin.
They wear what look like coats of
maps to cover up their skin.
They stretch up into the trees
the leaves to munch to bits,
And when they bend
to take a drink
they sort of do
the splits.

AjW

The answers

"When did the world begin and how?"
I asked a lamb, a goat, a cow:
"What's it all about and why?"
I asked a hog as he went by:
"Where will the whole thing end and when?"
I asked a duck, a goose, a hen:
And I copied all the answers too,
A quack, a honk, an oink, a moo.

Robert Clairmont

Way down south

Way down south where bananas grow,
A grasshopper stepped on an elephant's toe.
The elephant said, with tears in his eyes,
"Pick on somebody your own size."

Anonymous

OXFORD UNIVERSITY PRESS

Rhyming words are words that have the same sound.
For example: *shop/drop, door/four, eight/wait*

1 Make words that rhyme in the poems on page 58 the same colour. For example: *too/moo* (red)

2 Draw lines to match the words in box A that rhyme with the words in box B.

A

book

blue

mother

fairy

merry

bird

roar

throw

head

B

scary

word

zoo

ferry

go

cook

red

brother

pour

NOW TRY THIS!

Use rhyming words from the box to complete this limerick.

A man with a racing _____

Said, "I'm faster than you are."

His friend said, "Right!

Let's race _____!"

He did and he was faster by _____.

tonight

far

car

Monkey business

Read with your teacher.

I'd like to be a monkey

I'd like to be a monkey
    and swing from tree to tree,
I'd beat my chest and bare my teeth
    for all the world to see.
I'd like to be a monkey
    and eat bananas all day long,
Did you know that they are good for you?
    They make you smart and strong.
I'd like to be a monkey
    with ape-like things to do
But I wouldn't be a monkey
    if my home was in a zoo.

OXFORD UNIVERSITY PRESS

Some words are opposites. We call opposites antonyms.

1 Find words in the poem on page 60 that are opposites (antonyms) to these.

a weak _____

b bad _____

c night _____

d hate _____

Some words can mean the same or nearly the same as other words. These words are called synonyms.

2 Find words in the poem on page 60 that are synonyms for these.

a clever _____

b powerful _____

c slap _____

d consume _____

3 Write words from the poem on page 60 that rhyme with these words:

a tree _____

b strong _____

c do _____

d heart _____

NOW TRY THIS!

1 Write your own antonyms (opposites) for these words:

a dry _____

b big _____

c dirty _____

d empty _____

2 Circle the words that are synonyms for the **bold** word.

a weep	eat	good	cry	day
b shout	thin	yell	clean	large
c ape	open	ask	end	monkey

TOPIC 4: TEST YOURSELF!

Text cohesion and language devices

1 Shade the bubble next to the word that names this group of words: *sister, brother, mother, father, uncle, aunt.*

○ children   ○ family   ○ men   ○ women

2 Shade the bubble next to the word that names this group of words: *teacher, plumber, electrician, doctor, pilot.*

○ men   ○ women   ○ jobs   ○ family

3 Shade the bubbles next to the **two** synonyms (words with the same or nearly the same meaning).

○ run   ○ drop   ○ catch   ○ jog

4 Shade the bubble next to the antonym (opposite) of **heavy**.

○ light   ○ large   ○ strong   ○ huge

5 Shade the bubble next to the synonym for **sad**.

○ angry   ○ happy   ○ unhappy   ○ spoke

6 Shade the bubbles next to the **two** antonyms.

○ thin   ○ slow   ○ pick   ○ thick

7 Shade the bubbles next to the rhyming words.

○ cry   ○ flew   ○ high   ○ night

OXFORD UNIVERSITY PRESS

8 Cross out the word in each list that does not belong.

a bowl   dish   plate   pencil   basin

b saw   drill   bike   hammer   screwdriver

c park   street   road   lane   highway

9 Draw lines to match the antonyms.

fast   day   catch   throw

night   pull   slow   push

10 Draw lines to match the synonyms.

broom   ship   brush   plank

laugh   giggle   boat   board

HOW AM I DOING?

Colour the boxes if you understand.

Some words can be opposites. They are called antonyms. ☐

Some words can mean the same or nearly the same.
They are called synonyms. ☐   Some words rhyme. ☐

History Secrets

The baby Gobbles

no bath

Ticky

where rattle

?

Tocky

like doggy

Timmy

go walk

Boppy

bird tree

Tammy

push

Tommy

want lolly

Bippy and Bubby

no go sleep

Tucky

OXFORD UNIVERSITY PRESS

Some groups of words make more sense than others.

Using the pictures on page 64, name the baby Gobble who said:

1 "I don't want a bath." _____

2 "We would like a lolly please." _____

3 "Where is my rattle?" _____

4 "Can I go for a walk?" _____

5 "Look at the bird in the tree." _____

6 "I like the dog." _____

7 "I don't want to go to bed yet." _____

8 "Could you please give me a push?" _____

A sentence must make sense.

NOW TRY THIS!

Read each sentence below. In the table, write the parts of the sentence under the headings to show who (or what) did what, where, when or how.

a Dad and I went for a walk in the park.   **b** We walked very slowly.

c Yesterday, Mum came home.

Who or what?	Did what?	Where? When? OR How?
a Dad and I	_____	_____
b _____	_____	_____
c _____	_____	_____

Now write a sentence of your own.

_____

Greedy MacReedy

Read the story with your teacher.

Greedy MacReedy saw a jar full of lollies. He pushed his hand into the jar and he grabbed a huge fistful of the yummy lollies.

Greedy tried to pull his hand out of the jar but he found that it would not come out. The narrow neck stopped him.

Greedy would not let go of any lollies so his fist was stuck. He burst into tears and he made a terrible racket.

Mother MacReedy saw what Greedy had done. She did not ring for the fire brigade. She did not ring for the police and she did not ring for an ambulance.

Mother MacReedy just laughed and said, "Perhaps you should try taking half as many lollies, my lad, or you will remain stuck there all day."

OXFORD UNIVERSITY PRESS

We can join short sentences together to make more interesting, longer sentences. Words that join short sentences together are called conjunctions.

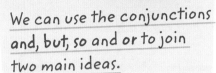

Use **and**, **but**, **so** or **or** to join each pair of sentences together to make one longer sentence from the story about Greedy MacReedy.

We can use the conjunctions and, but, so and or to join two main ideas.

Write your joined sentences on the lines.

1 He pushed his hand into the jar. He grabbed a huge fistful of the yummy lollies.

_____

_____

2 Greedy tried to pull his hand out of the jar. He found that it would not come out.

_____

_____

3 Greedy would not let go of any lollies. His fist was stuck.

_____

_____

4 "Perhaps you should try taking half as many lollies, my lad. You will remain stuck there all day."

_____

_____

NOW TRY THIS!

On a piece of paper, join two short sentences of your own using a conjunction such as **and**, **but**, **or** or **so**.

Bop's diary

Read with your teacher.

Today I woke up at seven. I got dressed, ate some Weet Bites and then I left for school.

In Grime Street I saw Tim waving to me. He was in his pyjamas.

"Ha, ha," I thought, "Tim will be late for school."

In Spotty Lane, Tock waved to me. Tock was still in her pyjamas.

"Ha, ha, Tock will be late, too."

In Mucky Road, Tick waved to me. He was in his pyjamas as well. Tick will be late, too.

When I started walking along Untidy Road, I saw Tam Tim.

She was getting the newspaper from her letterbox.

Tam was still in her pyjamas. Perhaps everyone is sick today.

When I got to Dusty Highway, I saw Bip Bip. Guess what?

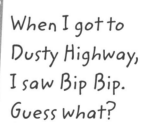

She was in her pyjamas, too.

"Hello Bop," she said, "You're up very early for a Saturday."

OXFORD UNIVERSITY PRESS

Proper nouns begin with a capital letter.
Sentences begin with a capital letter.
The word **I** is always written as a capital letter.

The names of people and places are called proper nouns.

1 Write these proper nouns with capital letters at the start.

a tock _____

b mucky road_____

c tam tim_____

d weet bites _____

2 Write these sentences with capital letters at the start.

a he was in his pyjamas. _____

b everyone is sick today. _____

c today I woke up at seven. _____

3 Write these sentences correctly.

a i got dressed and then i left for school.

_____

_____

b in grime street i saw tim waving to me.

_____

_____

NOW TRY THIS!

On a piece of paper, find and write the names and addresses of three different classmates. (Don't forget your CAPITALS!)

The pumpkin and the boy

Read this tall story from Africa with your teacher. It tells the story of a pumpkin, a boy and how the Earth and sky came to be.

There once was a great big pumpkin growing happily in a field on a hill. His name was Feegba, which means very big one. One day a boy came to the field to see if Feegba was ripe enough yet to put into a pot for pumpkin soup. The boy used his knife to scratch Feegba to see if he was ripe.

"I'm not ready yet," said Feegba.

The boy did not listen. He scratched deeper, thinking only of tasty pumpkin soup.

"I am not ready yet," said Feegba again.

The boy kept on scratching.

Feegba became very angry. He tore himself from his stalk. The startled boy began to run down the hill. Feegba chased the boy. The boy ran through a corn patch. Feegba flattened the corn patch. The boy ran through a pig herd. Feegba flattened the pigs. The boy ran through the village. Feegba flattened the village. The boy was about to collapse when he saw a shepherd with his sheep.

"Help me!" cried the boy.

"Do not fear, boy," said the shepherd. "My sheep, with their sharp horns, could stop the Moon."

The shepherd put his sheep into a line facing Feegba. When the pumpkin hit the line of sheep he split into two halves. One half became the Earth. One half became the sky. The pips became the stars and the pulp became the Milky Way.

That is one story about how the Earth and sky came to be.

Retold by AjW

OXFORD UNIVERSITY PRESS

Some sentences state a fact or give an opinion. They are called statements.
For example: *My dog is funny.* (opinion)
          His name is Jack. (fact)
Statements begin with a capital letter and end with a full stop.

1 Finish these statements from the story 'The pumpkin and the boy'.

> We can make longer statements by joining two main ideas with the conjunctions and, but, so and or.

a The boy did not _____ .

b The boy kept_____ .

c _____through the village.

d The shepherd put his_____

_____ .

e _____became the Earth.

Sometimes we can join two short sentences to make one longer sentence.
The boy kept on scratching. Feegba became very angry.
The boy kept on scratching and Feegba became very angry.

2 Make one sentence from these two.

The boy wanted to make pumpkin soup.

The pumpkin wasn't ripe enough.

_____

_____

NOW TRY THIS!

On another piece of paper, make one sentence by joining these two sentences.

It started to rain. We bought an umbrella.

Why did the children laugh?

Where do baby apes sleep?

In apricots.

How do you make a sausage roll?

It's easy: you push it.

Why did the turkey cross the road?

The chicken was on holiday.

How do you talk to a fish?

Drop it a line.

What colour is a shout?

Yell-Oh!

What has fur and whiskers and cuts grass?

A lawn meeeower.

Why was Cinderella a bad football player?

Her coach was a pumpkin.

OXFORD UNIVERSITY PRESS

Some sentences **ask** a question.

For example: *Where do you live? How old are you? What did you eat?*
When are you going home?

A question begins with a capital letter and ends with a question mark.

For example: *Can you see Tim yet?*

1 Write the questions that match these answers.
Remember to finish each question with a question mark.

a The chicken was on holiday.

_____

b In apricots.

_____

> To show that something is being asked, end a question with a question mark.

c Yell-Oh!

_____

d A lawn meeower.

_____

e Drop it a line.

_____

2 Write two questions that you could ask your friend.

_____

_____

NOW TRY THIS!

Write a joke of your own that asks a question.

_____

_____

The Gobbles at Funland

Read with your teacher.

The Gobbles are spending a day at Funland.

Tick rides on the THUNDER RIDE. It goes up and down and twists around. At the end of the ride Tick feels ill.

Look out!
Oh no!
Help!
Aargh!

Hooray!
Here we go!
Oh no!
Help!

Tock rides on the SPINNING JENNY. It goes around and around very fast. At the end of the ride Tock feels ill.

Look at me!
Ooh! No! No! No!
Yahoo!

Tim rides on the ZOOM ROCKET. It starts slowly and then suddenly goes very fast. At the end of the ride Tim feels ill.

Stop this at once!
This is fun!
Eeerk!

Tam rides on WHIPLASH. It goes around and around too. At the end of the ride Tam feels ill.

OXFORD UNIVERSITY PRESS

Some sentences show feelings. Sometimes these sentences are very short.
For example: *Aargh! Ooh!*
They can show someone is shouting a warning. For example: *Oh no! Look out!*
Some sentences shout orders. For example: *Let me off! Stop this at once!*
We use a mark like this **!** to end a sentence that shows feelings or shouts
an order.

1 Write two things that Tick said on the Thunder Ride.

_____

_____

2 Write two things that Tock said on the
Spinning Jenny.

_____

_____

A mark like this **!** is called an exclamation (say **ex-cluh-may-shun**) mark.

3 Write two things that Tim said on the Zoom Rocket.

_____

_____

4 Write two things that Tam said on Whiplash.

_____

_____

NOW TRY THIS!

Write a short sentence that:

- shouts an order _____

- shows a strong feeling _____

- is a shout of surprise _____

Collections

Here are some of the things that the Gobbles collect.

Tick collects cars and trucks. He collects fast cars, old cars, slow cars, big trucks and vans.

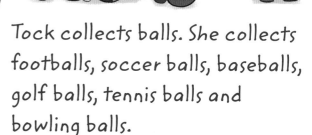

Tock collects balls. She collects footballs, soccer balls, baseballs, golf balls, tennis balls and bowling balls.

Tim collects cards. He collects monster cards, sports cards, dinosaur cards and playing cards.

Tam collects pets. She collects cats, dogs, rabbits, ducks and pigs.

Bip collects cakes. She collects cup cakes, chocolate cakes, fairy cakes and cream buns.

Bop collects coins. He collects 5-cent coins, 10-cent coins, 20-cent coins, 50-cent coins, $1 coins and $2 coins.

OXFORD UNIVERSITY PRESS

When we write a list in a sentence, we separate the words in the list with a comma.

For example: *In the fruit bowl was an apple, an orange, a banana and a peach.*

1 Write commas where they belong in these sentences.

a Tam collects cats dogs rabbits ducks and pigs.

b Tick collects fast cars slow cars big trucks and vans.

> There is no need for a comma to separate the second-last and last words in a list because and usually takes the place of a comma.

c Bip collects cup cakes chocolate cakes fairy cakes and cream buns.

d Lily's favourite sports are soccer netball basketball and swimming.

e At the zoo we saw lions tigers monkeys an elephant and a gorilla.

2 Complete this sentence about yourself, using commas where they belong.

My four favourite colours are _____

_____ and _____ .

NOW TRY THIS!

With his coins Bop wants to buy Bip four different presents.

Complete the sentence below to list what you think Bop might buy for Bip. Don't forget to use commas in your list.

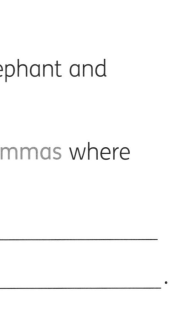

I think Bop will buy Bip_____

_____ and _____ .

At the zoo

OXFORD UNIVERSITY PRESS

Commas are often used to separate nouns (naming words) in a list.
For example: *On my table was a pen, a pencil, a marker and my book.*
Commas can also be used to separate a list of adjectives (describing words).
For example: *The cover of my book has green, yellow, red and blue stripes.*

The sentences below tell us which animals the Gobbles visited on their trip to the zoo. The commas are missing from the list of animals in each sentence.

1 Write the commas where they belong.

a Tim visited the bears monkeys gorillas possums and seals.

b Tock visited the camels giraffes lions and the Reptile House.

c Tam visited the Australian animals the cats and the elephants.

d Tick saw the birds the elephants an alligator and the apes.

e Bip and Bop went to see pandas bears cats and seals.

2 Use commas to separate the list of adjectives (describing words) in these questions.

a Which animal is huge grey four-legged and has a trunk?

b Can you name an animal that has stripes claws and sharp teeth?

c Are you going to buy that shiny blue sleeveless dress?

NOW TRY THIS!

On the zoo map on page 78, draw coloured lines to show the way each Gobble may have walked around the zoo to visit the animals.

Use orange for Tim, green for Tock, red for Tam, yellow for Tick and blue for Bip and Bop.

It's a fact!

Read these facts with your teacher.

Young koalas sometimes smell like cough lollies.

The hula hoop was used as a toy by Greek children thousands of years ago.

In Japan, watermelons are grown square. It is easier to stack them.

Did you know that rotten eggs float in water?

A finger lime is a citrus fruit that can be green, red, orange, yellow, purple, black or brown.

Dolphins have no sense of smell. They can see and hear very well.

OXFORD UNIVERSITY PRESS

1 Which of the following is a statement? Tick.

   a Did you know that rotten eggs float in water?

   b It's a fact!

   c Young koalas sometimes smell like cough lollies.

2 Use either **and**, **but** or **because** to join each pair of sentences to make one long sentence.

   a Dolphins have no sense of smell. They can see and hear very well.

   _____

   _____

   b In Japan, watermelons are grown square. It is easier to stack them.

   _____

   _____

3 Write the fact from page 80 that is a question.

   _____

4 Write the commas where they belong in this sentence.

   The finger lime is a citrus fruit that can be green red orange yellow purple black or brown.

NOW TRY THIS!

No lemons, no melon!

This exclamation is also a palindrome.

Use the clue to help you write what you think a palindrome might be.

Clue: Hannah, Bob and Tumut are also palindromes.

A palindrome is _____

TOPIC 5: TEST YOURSELF!

Sentences and punctuation

1 Shade the bubble next to the sentence that is correctly punctuated.

- ○ The children spent the day at the beach
- ○ The children spent the day at the beach.
- ○ The children spent the day at the beach?
- ○ The children spent the day at the beach!

2 Shade the bubble next to the sentence that is correctly punctuated.

- ○ Where did you buy your skateboard,
- ○ Where did you buy your skateboard.
- ○ Where did you buy your skateboard!
- ○ Where did you buy your skateboard?

3 Shade the bubble next to the punctuation mark that is missing from this sentence.

Look out Danny

○ .   ○ ?   ○ !   ○ ,

4 Write the missing punctuation marks in this sentence.

My favourite colours are red yellow green blue and pink.

OXFORD UNIVERSITY PRESS

5 In the text about cats below, draw:

- red circles around the full stops

- blue circles around the question marks

- red squares around the exclamation marks

- blue squares around the commas

and underline the capital letters.

It's all about cats!

A cat cannot move its jaw sideways.

Cats hate the smell of oranges, lemons, mandarins and grapefruit.

Common names for cats are Tabby, Smokey, Fluffy and Lucky.

What has fur and whiskers and cuts grass? A lawn meeower!

What do you call a man with cat scratches all over his face? Claude!

What is a cat's favourite colour? Purr-ple!

HOW AM I DOING?

Colour the boxes if you understand.

A sentence can be a statement, a question or an exclamation. ☐

Conjunctions can join short sentences together to make a longer sentence. ☐

I know when to use full stops, question marks and exclamation marks. ☐

How to grow sunflowers

Sunflowers are wonderful plants. They are easy to grow and, best of all, they grow very quickly! Some sunflower plants can grow to almost 3 metres tall!

Here's how to grow your own sunflowers.

What you need: a packet of sunflower seeds, compost, a digging tool, water, a ruler

What to do:

1   Find a sunny spot in the garden for your sunflower seeds.

2   Dig the area for your new garden bed.

3   Dig the compost into the soil.

4   Make small mounds of soil about 50 cm apart.

5   Plant five seeds half a centimetre deep in the top of each mound.

6   Water the seeds every day until the seedlings appear.

7   Remove the weakest plants so the strong plants have more room to grow.

OXFORD UNIVERSITY PRESS

Instructions usually start by listing the names (nouns) of things we need.
For example: *compost, a digging tool*

1 Read the instructions on page 84. Colour the nouns for things you will need. Use a different colour for each thing.

2 Write the noun group that names the most important thing you will need. _____

Instructions need to be easy to read. They usually include simple sentences as steps. The steps, in order, are commands telling what to do.

3 Complete these commands from the instructions on page 84.

a _____ a sunny spot in the garden.
(Hint: what action?)

b Dig _____ for your new garden bed.
(Hint: who or what?)

c _____ the compost _____ .
(Hint: what action?)   (Hint: where?)

d Make small mounds of soil _____ .
(Hint: where?)

e _____ every day.
(Hint: what action?)   (Hint: who or what?)

4 Step 7 uses the joining word **so** to join two main ideas. Underline each main idea joined by **so** in step 7.

NOW TRY THIS!

Add the missing capital letter and punctuation marks below.

sunflowers daisies daffodils roses and tulips are all flowers

The fox and the crow

Read with your teacher.

The crow sat in a tree with some cheese in her beak.

The quick fox jumped high trying to snatch the crow's cheese.

The clever fox found that he could not reach the crow so he thought of a plan.

"Oh Crow," he said. "You are so beautiful and so strong and so graceful. You are much prettier than that dull, old Peacock. Won't you please sing me a song so that I can say something nice about your voice?"

The crow was always looking for compliments so she opened her beak to sing.

The cheese fell to the ground. The fox quickly snatched it up saying, "You may be beautiful Crow, but I'm afraid you don't have much common sense. I am much smarter!"

Then he trotted off to enjoy his meal.

OXFORD UNIVERSITY PRESS

Stories (narratives) start with an opening sentence or sentences called an orientation (say *o-ree-en-tay-shun*). The orientation usually tells us who or what the story is about and where the story is taking place.

1 Name the two main characters introduced in the opening sentences of the story on page 86.

_____ and _____

Stories (narratives) often use lots of adjectives to describe or compare characters. For example: *prettier, smarter*

2 Complete the table by choosing adjectives from the box to match each character.

clever beautiful strong dull quick smarter graceful old

Fox	Crow	Peacock

3 Add the adjectives **prettier** or **smarter** to complete these sentences comparing characters in the story (narrative).

a The crow is much _____ than the peacock.

b The fox is _____ than the crow.

NOW TRY THIS!

On a piece of paper, add adjectives to the sentence below to create a longer, more interesting sentence. Include a joining word in your sentence.

I read a book _____.

Save our trees!

Read with your teacher.

Trees are very important to our world. We should plant more trees to save our environment.

First, experts agree that trees take in carbon dioxide and make oxygen. This helps to clean the air that we breathe.

Second, trees provide us with food and shelter. Our wildlife depends on forests, woods and jungles to provide the homes and food that they need to survive. In addition, we use the timber from trees to make strong, safe houses and beautiful furniture.

Finally, the roots of trees hold soil together. This stops the soil washing away. It also means soil isn't washed into our waterways so the water we drink stays clean.

Help save our environment! Get out and plant your favourite tree! What are you waiting for? You'll not only feel good, you'll help make the world a better, more beautiful place for the future!

OXFORD UNIVERSITY PRESS

When we write a text to persuade the reader to agree with us, we use the opening sentence or sentences to introduce the topic, give an opinion and state our position, for or against.

1 With your teacher, read the two opening sentences that give an opinion. Is the writer for or against planting trees? _____

Adjectives are often used in persuasive writing to describe the writer's opinion. For example: **good, better, wonderful**

Remember: Adjectives are describing words.

2 Tick the sentence in each pair that includes an adjective **that describes the writer's opinion**.

a   Trees are very **important**. ☐   Trees can be **big** or **small**. ☐

b   Trees are usually **green**. ☐   Trees are **beautiful**. ☐

c   This is an **Australian tree**. ☐   This is my **favourite** tree. ☐

Texts that argue a point often include exclamations to show strong feelings and questions to include the readers. For example: *I love trees!*

3 Find the exclamations in the text. How many are there? _____

4 Shade the bubble with the sentence that is correctly punctuated.

○ what are you waiting for?   ○ What are you waiting for.

○ What are you waiting for,   ○ What are you waiting for?

NOW TRY THIS!

Circle the words in each group that mean the same or nearly the same (synonyms) as the word in bold.

| **forest** | woods | furniture | jungle | roots |
| **home** | timber | cottage | house | school |

As busy as a bee

as strong as an _____

as slippery as an _____

as straight as an _____

as quiet as a _____

shaking like a _____

slept like a _____

OXFORD UNIVERSITY PRESS

A **simile** is a short group of words that show a likeness between two things.
For example: *as cold as ice, as soft as silk, slept like a log*

1 Use the words in the box to complete the **similes** on page 90.

> log eel jelly mouse ox arrow

2 Use the words in the box to complete the **similes** below.

> pretty cool black fit solid busy light

a as _____ as a cucumber

b as _____ as a fiddle

c as _____ as a picture

d as _____ as a feather

e as _____ as a bee

f as _____ as ink

g as _____ as a rock

We can use similes to make our writing more interesting.

NOW TRY THIS!

Underline the **similes** in these sentences.

a Ari was as brave as a lion.

b "My room is as clean as a whistle," said Rani.

c He was as cunning as a fox.

d After many lessons Charlie could swim like a fish.

UNIT 7.1   Verb tense

Then, now, later

Yesterday, Bip and Bop watched cricket.

Today Bip and Bop are playing cricket.

Tomorrow Bip and Bop will go to school.

Before lunch, dark clouds came over.

Now it is raining.

Soon the Sun will shine.

Last week Tick wrote a birthday card to Tock.

Today Tock is reading her birthday card from Tick.

Tonight Tock will phone Tick to thank him for the birthday card.

OXFORD UNIVERSITY PRESS

Sentences can tell us **when** things happen. The **verbs** or **verb groups** in each sentence give us clues about when things are happening.

For example: I *sat* in my chair. (past – *then*)

I *am sitting* in my chair. (present – *now*)

I *will sit* in my chair. (future – *later*)

1 Use page 92 to help you write a **verb** or **verb group** that tells what happened, what is happening and what will happen.

a What did Bop do **yesterday**? He _____ cricket.

b What are Bip and Bop doing **today**? They _____

_____ cricket.

c What will happen **tomorrow**? Bip and Bop _____

to school.

d What happened **before lunch**? Dark clouds _____ over.

e What is happening **now**? It _____ .

f What will happen **soon**? The sun _____ .

g What did Tick do **last week**? He _____ to Tock.

h What is Tock doing **today**?

She _____ Tick's birthday card.

i What will happen **tonight**?

Tock _____ Tick.

NOW TRY THIS!

On a piece of paper, write your own sentences:

- about something you did **yesterday**. Yesterday, I _____
- about something you are doing **now**. Now I am _____
- about something you will do **tomorrow**. Tomorrow I will _____

Knock, knock

Knock, knock 1

Tick

Knock, knock.

Who's there?

Nana.

Nana who?

Nana your business.

Tock

Knock, knock 2

Tim

Knock, knock.

Who's there?

Cowsgo.

Cowsgo who?

Cows go moo, not who.

Tam

Knock, knock 3

Bip

Knock, knock.

Who's there?

Shirley.

Shirley who?

Shirley you must know by now.

Bop

OXFORD UNIVERSITY PRESS

Saying verbs tell us how someone is speaking.
For example: *said*, *called*, *asked* and *shouted* are saying verbs.

1 Use 'Knock, knock 1' on page 94 to write **said** or **asked**.

"Knock, knock," _____ Tick.

"Who's there?" _____ Tock.

"Nana," _____ Tick.

"Nana who?" _____ Tock.

"Nana your business," _____ Tick.

2 Use 'Knock, knock 2' on page 94 to complete this knock, knock joke.

" _____ !" shouted Tim.

" _____ ?" asked Tam.

" _____ ," said Tim.

" _____ ?" asked Tam.

" _____ ," laughed Tim.

3 Write your own saying verb to complete these sentences.

a "Haha! You are very funny!" _____ Keegan.

b "Look out or it will hit you!" _____ Elly.

NOW TRY THIS!

Use questions I and 2 above to help you write out your own knock, knock joke. Use a separate piece of paper.

It's fun time!

I'm playing basketball!

She's a really good player.

She's riding her skateboard.

Wheeee! You can't catch me!

Why aren't you swimming?

It's freezing!

OXFORD UNIVERSITY PRESS

Sometimes we join two words together to make one shortened word (called a contraction).

An apostrophe of contraction (') takes the place of any letters that have been left out.

For example: *we're = we are* (the apostrophe replaces *a* in *are*)

1 Read 'It's fun time!' Colour all the words that have an apostrophe of contraction.

2 Can you write the full words in place of the contractions to finish these sentences from page 96?

a _____ playing basketball.

b _____ a really good player.

c _____ riding her skateboard.

d Wheeee! You _____ catch me!

e _____ freezing!

> Many contractions are formed from a verb and the word *not*. The *o* in *not* is replaced with an apostrophe.

3 Write the contractions that match the longer words below.

a is not _____

b was not _____

c has not _____

d did not _____

NOW TRY THIS!

Sometimes contractions are awkward if we write them in full.

For example: **Didn't** *you see me?* (**Did not**) *you see me?*

So instead we change the order of the words: **Did** *you* **not** *see me?*

How could we write the following question in full so that it makes sense?

Why aren't you swimming?

_____

Kitten and Mouse

Read with your teacher.

A story from Suriname

Long ago, Kitten and Mouse were good friends.

They played together all the time. They ran and jumped and scrambled and tumbled. They played Hide and Seek and Tag.

They were very happy.

One day when Mouse got home from a big play day his mother asked, "Who did you play with today?"

"Kitten," said Mouse.

"What?" said Mouse's mother. "You must never play with Kitten again. She's your enemy."

On that same day when Kitten got home her mother asked, "Who did you play with today?"

"Mouse," answered Kitten.

"What?" said Kitten's mother. "You must never play with Mouse again. He's your enemy."

The next day when Kitten and Mouse met, Kitten asked Mouse, "Do you want to play?"

"No," said Mouse sadly. "You're my enemy so I can't play with you."

Kitten and Mouse never played with each other again, but sometimes they both wished that they had never found out they were enemies.

OXFORD UNIVERSITY PRESS

1 Use verbs from the box to complete the following sentences from the story.

> play   tumbled   played   ran   were

a They _____ together all the time.

b They _____ very happy.

c "Who did you _____ with today?"

d They _____ and jumped and scrambled

and _____ .

2 Write saying verbs from the box to fill the gaps in the sentences below.

> shouted   asked   explained

a "Where are you going?"_____Bip.

b "Look out!" _____ Tock.

c "I have been playing with Mouse," _____Kitten.

3 Use the story to help you write these words as contractions.

a you are _____   b she is _____

c can not _____   d he is _____

NOW TRY THIS!

Can you write the missing word in each group?

a play   _____   playing

b jump   _____   jumped

c wishing   _____   wished

Using grammar

1 Shade the bubble that shows a noun group.

○ said Meg   ○ dig the garden
○ run quickly   ○ a book of puzzles

2 Shade the bubble with the adjective that best describes this character.

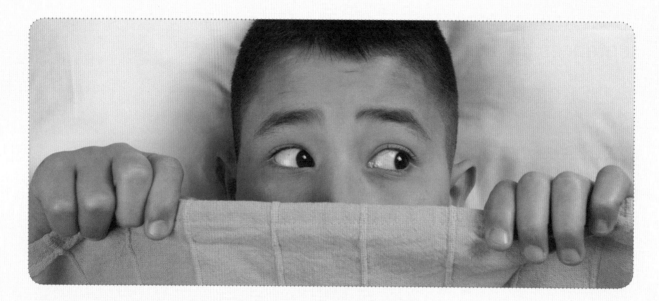

○ beautiful   ○ angry   ○ frightened   ○ sad

3 Shade the bubble that shows an opinion.

○ Whales are mammals.

○ Whales should not be hunted.

○ Whales eat krill.

○ Whales can be huge.

OXFORD UNIVERSITY PRESS

4 Shade the bubble with the best word to complete this simile.

as gentle as a _____

○ tiger   ○ goat   ○ lamb   ○ rattlesnake

5 Shade the bubble with the word or word group that would best finish this sentence.

Yesterday we _____ a funny movie.

○ will watch   ○ watched   ○ are watching   ○ am watching

6 Shade the bubble with the saying verb that would best finish this sentence.

"That's a very funny joke," _____ Eddie.

○ asked   ○ yelled   ○ wondered   ○ laughed

7 Shade the bubble that shows the correct contraction for **you are**.

○ y'are   ○ you're   ○ yo'ure   ○ your

8 Shade the bubble that shows the letter that has been left out of this contraction: **aren't**.

○ o   ○ a   ○ i   ○ t

TIME TO REFLECT

Tick each box when you can do the things listed.

☐ common nouns   I can use common nouns when I write sentences.

☐ proper nouns   When I write the proper nouns for people, places and things, I write them beginning with a capital letter.

☐ pronouns   I understand that words such as **I, he, she, we** and **they** can take the place of nouns.

☐ adjectives   I can use describing words when I write sentences.

☐ articles   I understand that **a, an** and **the** are often used in front of common nouns.

☐ noun groups   I know that articles and adjectives can be used with nouns to make noun groups.

☐ verbs and verb groups   My sentences always contain a word or words telling what is being done or what is happening.

☐ when, where and how words (adverbs and phrases)   I can use **when, where** and **how** words to add details to my sentences.

☐ antonyms   I can write opposites.

☐ synonyms   I can write words that mean the same or nearly the same.

☐ rhyming words   I can identify and use some rhyming words in my writing.

☐ sentences   I can write simple sentences and longer sentences.

☐ joining words (conjunctions)   I can use **and, but, so** and **or** to join two main ideas to make a longer sentence.

☐ capital letters and full stops   I use a capital letter to begin a sentence and a full stop (.) to end a sentence.

☐ question marks   I use a question mark (**?**) at the end of a question.

☐ exclamation marks   I use an exclamation mark (**!**) to show that someone is using a raised voice.

☐ commas   I use commas to separate items in a list.

OXFORD UNIVERSITY PRESS

GLOSSARY

adjective	A word that describes or tells us more about other words. *funny, messy, blue, one, round, big*
adverb	A word that tells when, where or how. *yesterday* (when), *here* (where), *quickly* (how)
antonym	An opposite. *full/empty, sitting/standing, front/back*
apostrophe of contraction	A mark similar to a comma that shows that a word has been shortened and has one or more letters missing. *can't, isn't, we'll, I'm, shouldn't*
article	The words *the, a* and *an*.
capital letter	An upper-case letter. *A B C D E F G H I J K L M N O P Q R S T U V W X Y Z*
comma	A punctuation mark (,) that shows a short break or pause in a sentence, separate words in a list or separate parts of a sentence.
conjunction	Also called a joining word. A conjunction is used to join other words or parts of a sentence.
exclamation	A sentence that expresses a raised voice or strong feeling. *Look out! Don't look yet!*
exclamation mark	The mark (!) that shows where an exclamation ends.
full stop	The mark (.) that shows us where a statement ends. *Last week Tick wrote to Tock.*
noun	A word that names people, places, animals, things or ideas. Nouns can be: abstract nouns (things that cannot be seen or touched): *happiness, idea* common nouns (names of ordinary things): *hat, toys, pet, mouse, clock, bird* proper nouns (special names): *Zoe, Jack, Monday, January, Easter, Australia* technical nouns (sometimes called scientific nouns): *oxygen*

noun group	A group of words, often including an article, an adjective and a noun, built around a main noun. *the big, black car*
phrase	A group of words that tells us how, when or where. *in the car, after lunch, with a spoon, under the bridge*
preposition	A word that usually begins a phrase. *on, in, over, under, before, after, between*
pronoun	A word that can take the place of a noun to represent a person, place or thing. *he, she, I, it, they, we, us, me, them, mine*
question	A sentence that asks something. *Is Tock hiding under the bed?*
sentence	A group of words, containing at least one verb, that makes sense. A simple sentence has one main idea and one verb or verb group: *The birds were sitting on the fence.* A compound sentence uses *and, but, or, so* to join two main ideas. A compound sentence has two verbs or verb groups. *Some birds were sitting on the fence and a cat was lurking below.*
statement	A sentence that states facts or gives opinions. *The horse ran around the paddock.* *I like ice cream.*
synonym	A word that means the same or nearly the same as another word. *shouts/yells, thin/skinny*
verb	A word that tells us what is happening or what is being done in a sentence. Verbs can be: doing verbs: *throw, sit* relating verbs: *am, is, are, was, were, has, have, had* saying verbs: *said, whispered* thinking and feeling verbs: *know, like*

OXFORD UNIVERSITY PRESS